OCT 1992

Amazing
Boats

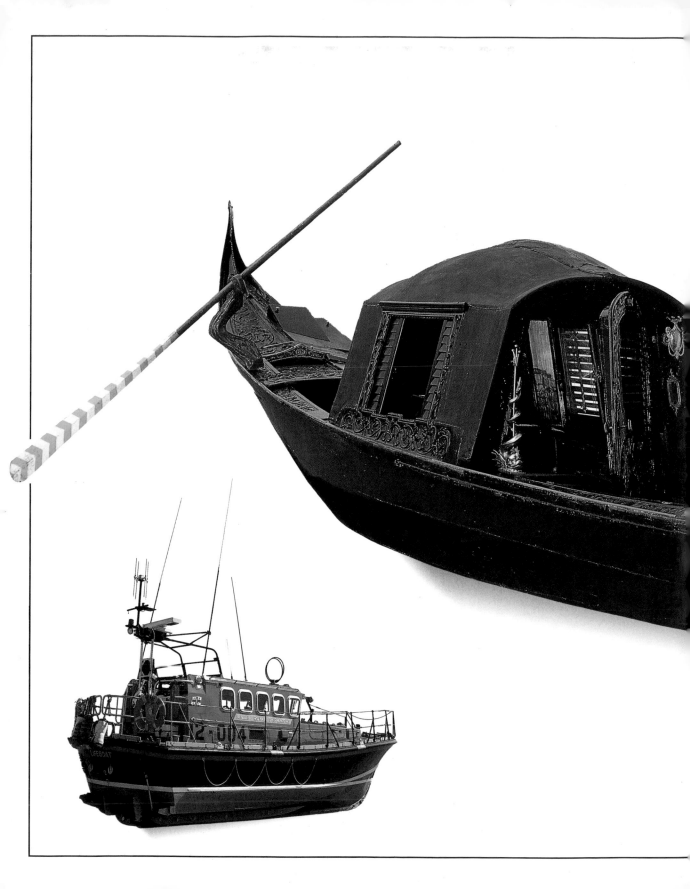

EYEWITNESS JUNIORS

Amazing Boats

WRITTEN BY
MARGARETTE LINCOLN

PHOTOGRAPHED BY
MIKE DUNNING
& RAY MOLLER

ALFRED A. KNOPF • NEW YORK

DK

Conceived and produced by
Dorling Kindersley Limited

Editor Bernadette Crowley
Art editor Hans Verkroost
Managing editor Sophie Mitchell
Managing art editor Miranda Kennedy
Production Shelagh Gibson

Illustrations by Peter Dennis and Julie Anderson
Boats supplied by International Sailing Craft Association (pp 8-9, 10-11, 14-15, 22-23, 26-27);
Windermere Steamboat Museum and Motorboat Collection (pp 12-13);
The Exeter Rowing Club (pp 16-17); Hastings Lifeboat Station (pp 20-21);
Penton Hook Boat Marine Sales (pp 24-25); Simon Geer (pp 28-29)
Special thanks to David Fung and Carl Gombrich for research,
and to Tim Barker, David Goddard, Steve Martin, and Paul Wilson
for their help in finding the boats for photography

The publishers would like to thank Pickthall Picture Library/Tom for their kind
permission to reproduce the main photograph on the cover and on pp 18-19
The author would like to dedicate this book to Sophie

This is a Borzoi Book published by Alfred A. Knopf, Inc.

First American edition, 1992

Manufactured in Italy   0 9 8 7 6 5 4 3 2 1

Library of Congress Cataloging in Publication Data
Lincoln, Margarette.
Amazing boats / written by Margarette Lincoln;
photographed by Mike Dunning and Ray Moller.
p. cm. – (Eyewitness juniors; 21)
Includes index.
Summary: Text and photos provide an introduction to the history of
boats, from simple floating logs and dugout canoes to high-tech
fishing boats, icebreakers, and floating airports.
1. Boats and boating – History – Juvenile literature.
2. Navigation – History – Juvenile literature.
[1. Boats and boating – History.] I. Dunning, Mike, ill.
II. Moller, Ray, ill. III. Title. IV. Series.
VM150.L49   1992   623.8'202 – dc20   92-3045
ISBN 0-679-82770-6
ISBN 0-679-92770-0 (lib. bdg.)

Color reproduction by Colourscan, Singapore
Printed in Italy by A. Mondadori Editore, Verona

Contents

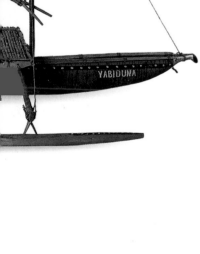

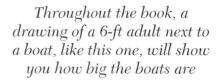

Throughout the book, a drawing of a 6-ft adult next to a boat, like this one, will show you how big the boats are

First boats

Boats were invented thousands of years ago. People noticed that certain materials, like wood and reed, floated on water. So they used these materials to carry themselves across the water.

Digging in

People hollowed out logs to make canoes called dugouts. They used tools of pointed stone, bronze, and later, iron. Sometimes they used fire to burn into the log and make cutting easier

Travel by tree!

The first boats were probably just large logs. But logs turn over easily. To keep them from rolling, several logs were tied together to make a raft.

Hide boat

Some early boats, such as the coracle, were made from animal skin stretched over a wood frame. Coracles are still used for fishing in Wales and Ireland, but they are now made of a thick cotton cloth called calico.

Coracles can be carried across the back

Reed boats

Early Egyptians made boats by tying bundles of reeds together. Reed boats are still used in some countries. This reed boat is used by fishermen on Lake Titicaca in Peru.

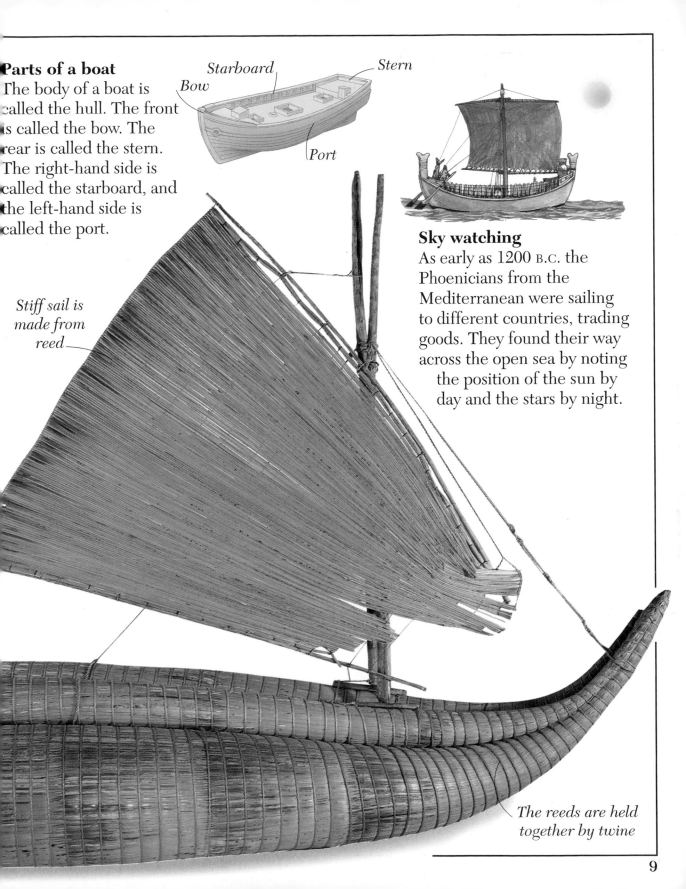

Parts of a boat
The body of a boat is
called the hull. The front
is called the bow. The
rear is called the stern.
The right-hand side is
called the starboard, and
the left-hand side is
called the port.

Starboard

Bow

Stern

Port

Sky watching
As early as 1200 B.C. the
Phoenicians from the
Mediterranean were sailing
to different countries, trading
goods. They found their way
across the open sea by noting
the position of the sun by
day and the stars by night.

*Stiff sail is
made from
reed*

*The reeds are held
together by twine*

Canoeing & rafting

Canoes and rafts are the simplest boats, but they can stay afloat in the roughest of waters.

Canoes at war
The Maori people of New Zealand went to war in large dugout canoes. These canoes were long and narrow and traveled very fast.

Wriggling raft
Whitewater rafting is a sport in which crews paddle inflatable rubber boats through rapids, or rough parts of a river. The rubber boats twist and wriggle as if they were made of jelly.

Cold canoes
The Inuit people in the Arctic made canoes for hunting sea mammals, such as seals. These canoes, called kayaks, were made of sealskins sewn together around a wood frame.

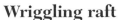

This boat is from Indonesia and is used for fishing and for sporting competitions between villages

Bark canoes
Native Americans used to make canoes out of sheets of tree bark. The sheets of bark were sewn together using thread made from tree roots. Wood ribs gave the canoe shape and strength.

The oar is used as a rudder

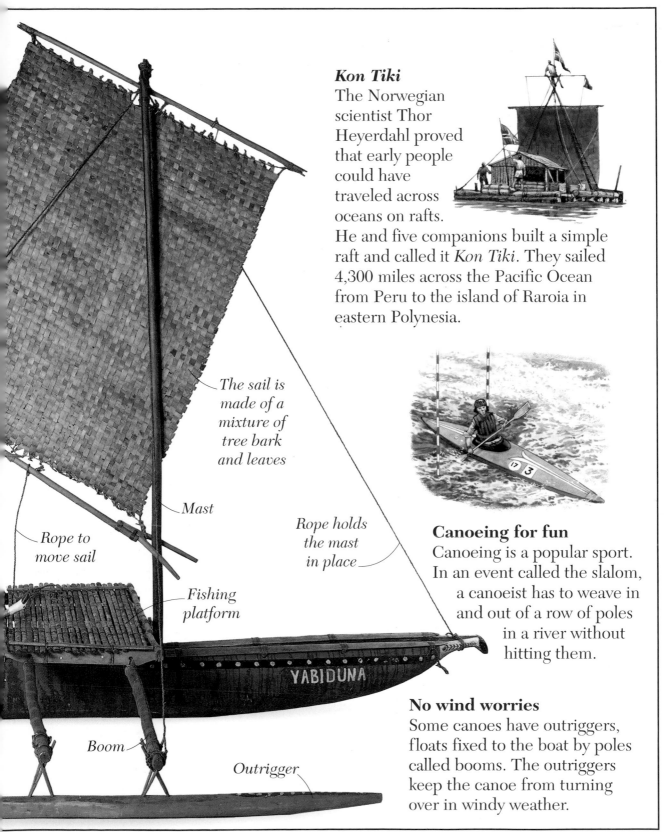

Kon Tiki

The Norwegian scientist Thor Heyerdahl proved that early people could have traveled across oceans on rafts.
He and five companions built a simple raft and called it *Kon Tiki*. They sailed 4,300 miles across the Pacific Ocean from Peru to the island of Raroia in eastern Polynesia.

The sail is made of a mixture of tree bark and leaves

Mast

Rope holds the mast in place

Rope to move sail

Fishing platform

Boom

Outrigger

YABIDUNA

Canoeing for fun

Canoeing is a popular sport. In an event called the slalom, a canoeist has to weave in and out of a row of poles in a river without hitting them.

No wind worries

Some canoes have outriggers, floats fixed to the boat by poles called booms. The outriggers keep the canoe from turning over in windy weather.

Full steam ahead!

When the steam engine was invented in the late 1700s, it was put into boats to turn paddle wheels and propellers. Paddle wheels have big blades that push the water behind them and move the boat forward.

Burning ambition

In 1838 *Sirius* was the first steamship to cross the Atlantic without using sails. It ran out of fuel before the end of its journey and made the last few miles by burning its wood furniture and doors – and one of its masts – to raise enough steam to keep the engine going!

Steam along

This elegant steamboat was built in 1896 for pleasure trips and tea parties on Lake Windermere in England. It is still steaming along today taking visitors for trips on the lake.

Up the Mississippi

Steam-powered paddle wheelers carried passengers and freight before there were trains. Steamboats on the Mississippi River had a flat hull because they had to pass through very shallow sections of the river.

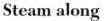

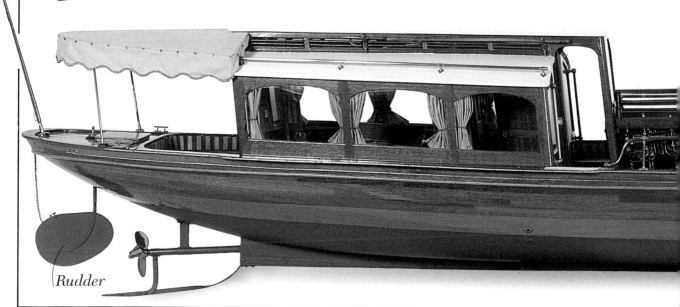

Rudder

Wind speed

In 1895 the crew of the steamship *Tuapehu* watched in amazement as it was overtaken by the sailing ship *Turakina* in stormy weather. This showed that, in the right weather conditions, the force of the wind can be greater than the force of an engine.

Heave-ho!

In 1845 a tug of war was held between two ships to see if propeller power was greater than paddle power. With both ships on full steam, the propeller-driven *Rattler* easily pulled the paddleboat *Alecto*.

Follow the leader

Paddleboats are handy for towing ships into harbors and ports. They can stop more quickly than a propeller-driven boat, reverse almost as easily as go forward, and make sharp turns by going forward on one wheel and backward on the other.

Made of iron

The steamship *Great Britain*, built in 1843, was the first large passenger ship to be made of iron and the first one to use a propeller, not a paddle. It had sails and masts – just in case the engine failed.

Steam from engine comes out through funnel

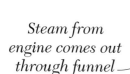

Fishing boats

Fishing boats come in all sorts of amazing shapes and sizes. Some are simple wooden rowboats; others carry computers and radar to help them find fish.

Stacking system
Fishing boats called dories were used in Newfoundland, Canada, until the 1940s. They were stacked on a big ship and carried to fishing grounds where fishermen would lower them into the sea. At the end of the day the ship would collect them.

Egyptian fishing
The ancient Egyptians fished on the Nile River. Their boats were made of papyrus reeds, a plant that grows along the Nile. To catch fish, two boats would row side by side, linked together by a net. The net scooped up fish as the boats traveled along.

Jukung with sail up

Island fishing boat
This brightly colored fishing boat is a dugout canoe called a *jukung*. It is from Madura, a small island in Indonesia.

Outrigger to balance canoe

Fishing by helicopter

Modern tuna-fishing boats carry
a helicopter. The helicopter flies
ahead of the boat to spot groups
of tuna swimming below.

Fishing spirits

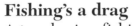

Many years ago, in
certain countries,
fishing boats often
had two eyes painted
on the front of them.
This was because the fishermen believed
that boats had spirits and the eyes allowed
the boats to see where they were going.

Fishy lady

Some fishermen have reported
seeing mermaids – creatures half
human and half fish. In 1825 a
mermaid from Japan was brought
to London, England. But she was
found to be a fake – a woman with
a fish's tail sewn to her skin!

Fishing's a drag

A trawler is a fishing boat that
drags a huge net behind it.
Long ropes allow the net
to catch fish that
live near the
bottom of
the sea.

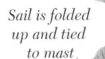

*Sail is folded
up and tied
to mast*

Rudder

Rowboats

People first moved their boats along by paddling with their hands. Later, paddles and oars were invented to move boats faster and help steer them. Paddles are smaller than oars and are used for light boats. Heavier boats need the stronger oars to move them.

Viking venturers
The Vikings, from northern Europe, built light, fast rowboats. Vikings sailed the seas between 800 A.D. and 1200 A.D., and even reached North America. They must have gotten cold and wet in their open boats.

The coxswain sits here

Shoes for the rowers are attached to the boat

The boat is made of fiberglass

Each rower pulls one oar

Rowboat racing
This rowboat is used for racing. When people row, they sit backward. The seats slide as the rowers row; this action gives more power to each stroke, or pull of the oars. A person known as a coxswain (*cox'n*) steers the boat and makes sure everyone rows together.

Rebellion at sea
In 1789 most of the crew of a ship called *Bounty* rebelled against their captain, William Bligh. He and 18 loyal men were set adrift in a small rowboat. They had little food, no charts, and suffered terrible cold and hunger. After 43 days they found land, having traveled 3,900 miles.

Oars across the ocean

In 1972 John Fairfax and Sylvia Cook were the first to row across the Pacific Ocean. During their 8,000-mile journey in their boat, *Brittania II*, they survived a hurricane, were shipwrecked off an island, and were attacked by a shark – John Fairfax was badly bitten on his arm.

Fishy way to travel

The Chinese have small boats called sampans. They steer the boats and propel them, or move them forward, with a long oar over the stern. The oar is called a *yuloh*. To propel the boat, the *yuloh* is moved from side to side like a fish's tail.

Seats are on wheels and slide along rails

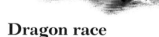

Grecian galleys

The ancient Greeks went to war in ships called galleys. The oarsmen were usually seated on three different levels so their oars would not clash, and they rowed in time to tunes played on a flute!

Dragon race

Every year, a dragon boat festival is held in Hong Kong. Dragon boats are huge canoes each rowed by about 20 people. The highlight of the festival is a race in which over 40 dragon boats compete.

Sailboats

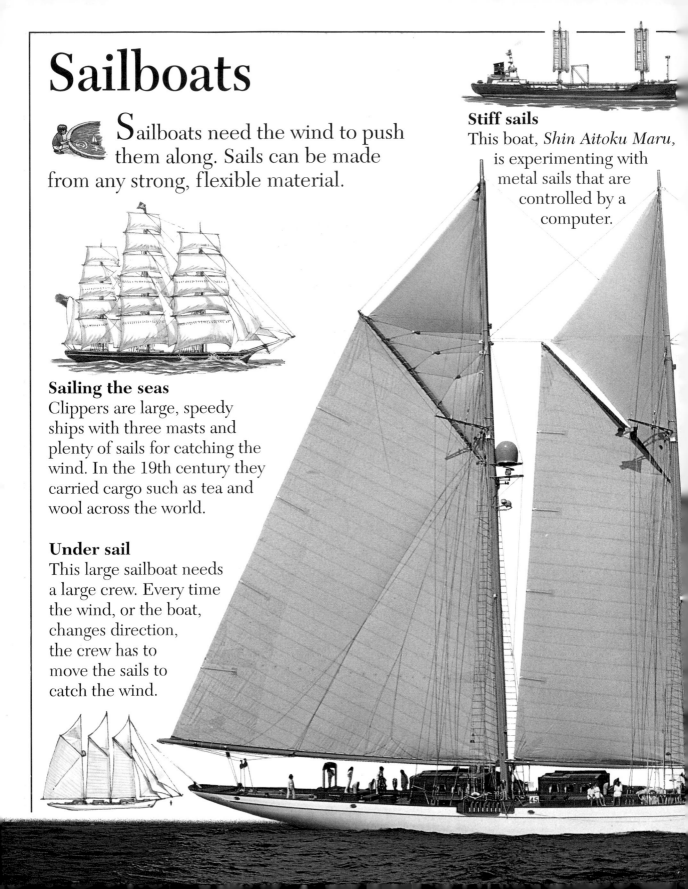

Sailboats need the wind to push them along. Sails can be made from any strong, flexible material.

Sailing the seas
Clippers are large, speedy ships with three masts and plenty of sails for catching the wind. In the 19th century they carried cargo such as tea and wool across the world.

Under sail
This large sailboat needs a large crew. Every time the wind, or the boat, changes direction, the crew has to move the sails to catch the wind.

Stiff sails
This boat, *Shin Aitoku Maru*, is experimenting with metal sails that are controlled by a computer.

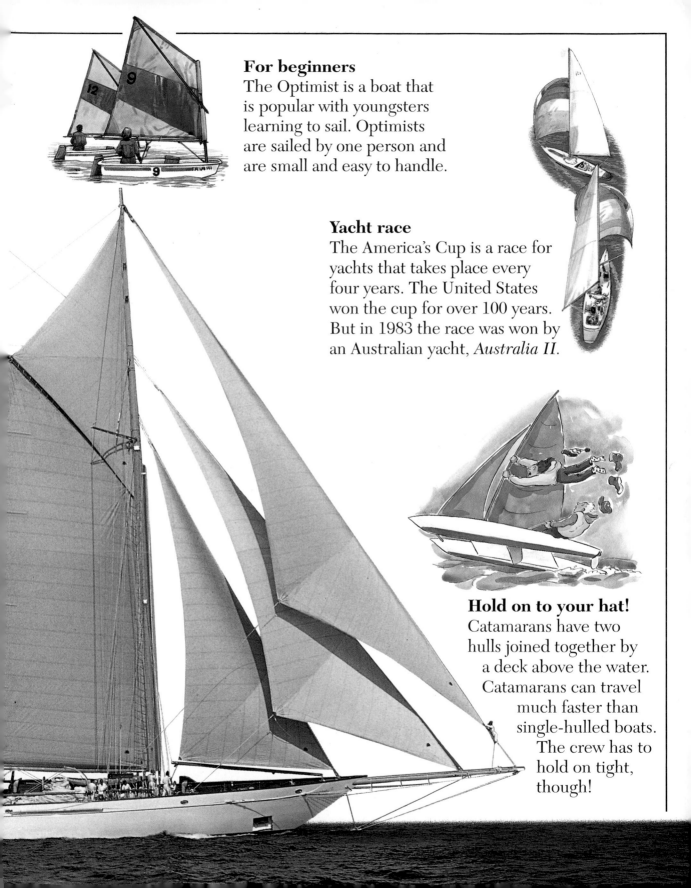

For beginners
The Optimist is a boat that is popular with youngsters learning to sail. Optimists are sailed by one person and are small and easy to handle.

Yacht race
The America's Cup is a race for yachts that takes place every four years. The United States won the cup for over 100 years. But in 1983 the race was won by an Australian yacht, *Australia II*.

Hold on to your hat!
Catamarans have two hulls joined together by a deck above the water. Catamarans can travel much faster than single-hulled boats. The crew has to hold on tight, though!

Lifeboats

Lifeboats are specially built for saving lives at sea and are almost unsinkable. United States and Canadian Coast Guard lifeboats stand ready to help rescue any person or boat in trouble.

Radiotelephone antenna

Radar

Rules of the road
A waterway is like a road, but for boats. Boats must keep to the right on a waterway. At night, or in fog, boats carry a red light on the port side and a green light on the starboard side.

Radio antennas receive distress signals

Searchlight

Making a splash
Lifeboats are launched as quickly as possible. They slide down a slipway leading from their shed to the sea.

This British lifeboat carries a crew of six

R.N.L.B. ROYAL SHIPWRIGHT

12-004

The body is made of aluminum

Men against the sea
Early lifeboats had no engine or radio, just oars and sails. Their brave crews were in great danger in rough seas.

Fancy that!
The crew of a ship stranded on an island in Scotland got quite a surprise when they were rescued by a viking, a clown, a jester, and a lion. The rescuers were volunteer lifeboatmen called out from a masquerade party!

Titanic disaster
In 1912 the *Titanic* was the largest ship ever built. It hit an iceberg on its first voyage. It was thought to be unsinkable and did not carry enough lifeboats for all its passengers. Of the 2,200 people on board, only 705 were saved.

It's unsinkable
A lifeboat won't sink because air is trapped in the cabin on the top of the boat. If the lifeboat capsizes, or turns upside down, the weight of its engines pulls the hull back into the water, and the boat is then right side up again.

Horn

Gliding along

A boat with an engine goes much faster than a boat without an engine. But gliding slowly along a river, without a noisy motor, makes boating a peaceful pleasure.

Swanning along

This elegant boat, shaped like a swan, was built in 1880. Dinner parties for up to 16 people were held on board the "swan" as it glided along the river.

Watery roads

Venice is a city with no roads and therefore no cars. Instead of roads, the city has hundreds of canals and narrow walkways. The only way to travel around Venice is on foot or by boat.

Canal cruiser

The graceful gondola is used in the canals of Venice, Italy. It is used for pleasure trips, and also as a taxi. In Venice, gondolas must be painted black – by law.

This gondola has a hood and is decorated with gold ornaments. These trimmings are put on for a ceremony, such as a wedding.

One person, called a gondolier, stands here to work the oar

Stern

The oar, called a sweep, propels and steers the gondola

Mandarin's boat

Many centuries ago in China important people in the government called mandarins had pleasure boats. They entertained friends on river trips while two oarsmen, working one large oar, gently moved the boat along.

Any requests?

Barges built to carry royalty are known as state barges. In the late 18th century the king of Thailand's state barge had two men to steer it and 50 men to paddle it. The king had a singer on board to entertain him on long journeys.

Pole pusher

Flat-bottomed boats called punts are used for gliding along rivers. One person propels the boat by pushing against the riverbed with a long pole.

Fit for a prince

This beautiful state barge was built in 1732 for Frederick, Prince of Wales. The prince sat in the part that looks like a coach. The detailed carving is covered with a thin layer of real gold.

All gondolas have this metal fitting, called a ferro, at the bow

The gondola has a wood hull

Motorboats

It is exciting to travel in a motorboat. Motorboats can go fast, and the biggest and most powerful ones can speed across an ocean.

That's the spirit
In 1978 a jet-propelled speedboat, *Spirit of Australia*, set a world water-speed record when it reached just over 319 mph.

Shaped for speed
The Pachanga 27 is designed for speed. Long journeys are no problem in this boat. There is a bed, two seats, a table, and a small kitchen inside the hull.

Race for power
Powerboats are designed for racing. The fastest have jet engines. In the Venice-Monte Carlo competition, powerboats race 1,320 miles around the coast of Italy.

Keeping above water
A hydrofoil is a boat with underwater wings, or foils. At high speed, the foils move upward, raising the hull of the boat out of the water. The hydrofoil can travel very fast and smoothly.

Towing the line

Water-skiers are towed along by motorboats. Often there are ramps in the water. Skiers slide up the ramps and fly through the air before landing again.

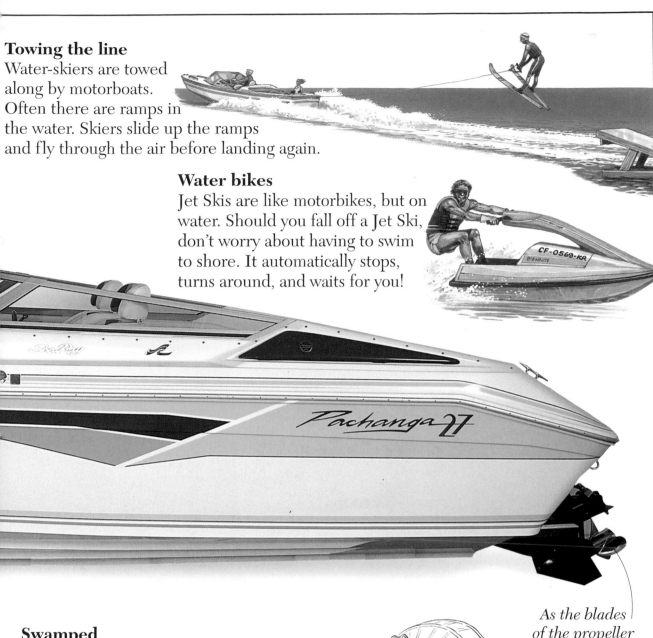

Water bikes

Jet Skis are like motorbikes, but on water. Should you fall off a Jet Ski, don't worry about having to swim to shore. It automatically stops, turns around, and waits for you!

Pachanga 27

Swamped

Swamp cruisers are flat-bottomed motorboats. The engine and propeller are mounted high up, allowing the boats to travel across the shallow waters of swamps and marshes.

As the blades of the propeller turn, they push the water backward, and the boat is thrust forward

Working boats

Working boats are special boats – they perform jobs. Some of them work to help other boats do *their* jobs.

The boat to catch
Ferry boats carry passengers, cars, and trucks across rivers and seas. Some ferries have railroad tracks in them and carry trains.

Bamboo rods hold the sails together

Breaking the ice
In places with very cold winters, rivers and harbors freeze. There are special boats called icebreakers that keep these waters clear for other boats. They have very strong hulls that can push through the ice.

Digging deep
Dredgers spend their lives in harbors and channels scooping up silt from the seabed and dumping it elsewhere. This keeps the water deep enough for big ships to sail in.

Smugglers beware
Illegal goods are often smuggled into countries on boats. Police boats patrol coastal waters on the lookout for any smugglers at work.

At one time, the junk was used as a warship by the Chinese

Junk
The junk is a flat-bottomed, ocean-going boat from the Far East. Junks were first built about 1,000 years ago. They carried goods for trading around the Pacific and Indian oceans.

Living on a boat

There are people who spend most of their lives on water. Some people would rather have a home on water than one on land.

Bangkok houseboats
In Bangkok, Thailand, people have lived on houseboats for centuries. The owners often use their houseboats as shops from which to sell food to passersby.

Life on a canal boat
In Britain in the last century, some families lived and worked on boats called narrow boats. The boats were brightly painted with pictures of roses and castles but the families were often overcrowded in their boat homes.

Straight and narrow
This boat is a narrow boat. Narrow boats were originally built to carry heavy goods along English canals. Today they are used mostly for vacation homes.

Floating airports
An aircraft carrier is a huge ship with a runway for aircraft. With a crew of more than 5,000 people, it is like a floating city. There is a hospital, a post office, a daily newspaper – and a jail, should anyone misbehave!

Kashmiri houseboats
In Kashmir, in the far north of India, there are "hotel houseboats" on the lakes. Some are luxury hotels with shaded sundecks and plush interiors.

Two by two
In a Bible story, God told Noah to build a big boat, called an ark. God said it was going to rain for 40 days and 40 nights, and there would be great floods in which all life on earth would die. Noah took his family and two of every kind of animal to live on the ark until the rain and floods stopped.

This narrow boat has four beds, a kitchen, a bathroom, and an area for dining

Tiller for moving the rudder by hand